How to Turn Stress on Its Head

the simple truth *that can change your relationship with work*

Dr RANI BORA

This book or any portion thereof
may not be reproduced or used in any manner whatsoever
without the express written permission of the publisher
except for the use of brief quotations in a book review.

Published in Great Britain

First Edition, 2017

For enquiries contact:
mail@ranibora.com

Visit the author's website at
https://ranibora.com

Cover design & formatting by
Suraj Gogoi

Dr Rani Bora has written a fascinating, eminently practical book that pulls back the curtains on how the human mind really works and in doing so, makes it possible for every human being to realize their innate health and well-being. The psycho-spiritual principles she describes and illustrates through real life stories make it possible and inevitable for every reader to experience greater freedom in all dimensions of life, including the demanding domain of work. This will be an extremely helpful resource for those who are seeking to transform their experience of life and work, all from the inside out!

- **Ian M Crooks**, MD, psychiatrist in Austin, Texas USA, and presenter of *The Doctor Is Within: Health, Happiness and Well-being.*

This little book will help you learn more about yourself, about what makes you tick and how to tick better. Rani illuminates the topic of mind, stress, anxiety and thought in a refreshing and new way, to enable us to see clearly what will have escaped most of us before. Reading this book, and absorbing the wisdom within will help you in your way forwards in Life to be more effortless and stress-free - by understanding the true source of our thinking. Thank you Rani!

- **Dr Andrew Tresidder** MBBS DRCOG MRCGP Cert Med Ed.

This book is what the healthcare field has been waiting for! The epidemic of stress and burnout is taking its toll on the helping profession! As a nurse for over 40 years, I can personally attest to the power of learning about the true source of stress (it's an inside job!) and about how the mind works. What you'll learn in this book is unlike anything else out there because this book does not offer what to do but instead offers an understanding. Are you ready to stress less? Then this book is for you! Rani provides hope and a simple solution for eliminating stress. Enjoy!

- **Karen Miller Williams**, *Three Principles Nurse, Life Coach, Consultant, Speaker.*

I wish I had this book with me when I was a Psychiatric Tutor responsible for training doctors to pass the membership exam of the Royal College of Psychiatrists. As a tutor and later as a Medical Director in my trust, I've seen first-hand the impact of stress not only on patients but also on trainees and health professionals. Dr Rani Bora helps us in understanding that a new metaphor based on an understanding of innate mental health and well-being is the next development for a 21st Century program for mental Health Professionals. Truly a paradigm shift in awareness of the logic of the psyche.
- **Dr William Hughes**,
MB BS, MRCS, LRCP, FRCPsych. Retired Medical Director of *Norfolk Mental Health Care Trust*
Member *International Association of Analytical Psychology*,
Founder Member *European Society for Dissociation* and Trauma,
Currently Consultant to *Village Coaching Network.*

If you have been trying to tackle stress at work or at home and failing then this book is worth a read. In an easy to read style Rani explains the *power of thought* and the effect this has on the way we feel. It's not necessarily psychology that will suit everyone on first reading, but I would encourage people to read this book and explore this understanding in more detail. It's not a quick fix solution to stress, but thought provoking and may help the reader develop better resilience to stress.
- **Dr Frances Forest**, Consultant Anaesthetist

The wonderful descriptions and examples in this book bring clarity and simplicity to what we all can recognise to be true about the human experience, but often find it difficult to express or think about. What Dr Rani Bora has shared in these pages is certainly a game changer for understanding mental health and stress in the workplace and in life - it has been for me personally. I honestly don't know anyone who wouldn't get value from finding a quiet space to really digest the message of this book and then dip back into it from time to time! As someone who has worked in the field of mental health for a couple of decades and has a lifelong commitment to changing the experience of people who are suffering with mental disorder for the better, I feel this book is a part of a larger tidal wave of change in the field, which will bring hope and transformation in the years to come.

- **Andrew (Andy) Smith**, *Transformative Coach, Trainer &*
Senior Community Acute Mental Health Services Manager, Camden and Islington NHS Foundation Trust

Dr Rani Bora shines a light on the incredible resilience and mental health within us all. In a beautifully simple way she explains a simple truth behind our minds ability to self-correct from stress. It might look like we need to fix our manager, boss or workload - but actually the answer is inside. If you, a friend or a colleague is experiencing work related stress then buy them this book.

- **Liz Scott**, *Well-being and Leadership Coach*

A thought provoking and refreshing approach to thinking about dealing with stress in the workplace...

- John Woolner, *UKCP Couple and Family Systemic Psychotherapist/Trainer*

Rani Bora's book is a valuable addition to the field of innate health and resilience. Through exploring the source of stress and its particular association in the workplace, Bora introduces the reader to a vital understanding of *the way the mind works*. A number of personal stories then provide real-life illustrations of how that new understanding has transformed how people experience their lives. The book is easy to read, accessible and provides a helpful resource to those who want to learn more about this developing field, as well as those already immersed.

- **Anthony Kessel**, Honorary Professor, *London School of Hygiene & Tropical Medicine*

This is a really helpful book for anybody, but I found it particularly relevant as a practising clinician and NHS manager. Rani explains the principles underlying this way of thinking very clearly and the *case histories* really bring the principles alive. I look forward to dipping into this little book on a regular basis for inspiration when my thinking leads me to experience stress in the moment!

- **Dr Jo Leahy**, Clinical Chair, *Telford & Wrekin CCG*

To my mother, my late father and family
for all your love and support...
To our friends and well-wishers
blessed to have a place in your hearts...

CONTENTS

INTRODUCTION   xi

Personal note from the author   *xi*
What this book is about   *xix*
Why should you care to learn this   *xx*
A few words of caution…   *xxvii*

Part ONE: Stress and Anxiety   1

Chapter 1: Is the real source of our stressful and anxious feelings 'out there'?   *3*
Chapter 2: What's the True Source of Stress and Anxiety in the workplace?   *9*
Chapter 3: Where do Feelings come from?   *13*
Chapter 4: Why what we Think Appears Real   *21*

Part TWO: The self-correcting system   27

Chapter 5: Our Psychological Immune System   *29*
Chapter 6: The Nature of Thought   *37*
Chapter 7: Implications of understanding innate psychological health and resilience   *43*

Part THREE: States of Mind   47

Chapter 8: Bringing out the best in you   *49*
Chapter 9: The space for reflection   *57*
Chapter 10: Self-management or self-regulation are quick fixes at best   *63*
Chapter 11: Dealing with 'difficult' people at work   *71*

Part FOUR: FAQs   77

Can my boss and colleagues make me feel stressed?   *79*
Are you saying that I should allow other people in power to use me 'as a doormat'?   *79*
So, am I the one making myself stressed?   *80*

Can I practice meditation or mindfulness to alleviate feelings of stress and anxiety at work? 82
But, I have a diagnosis of mental health/physical health issues that hinder me being my best at work. 82

Part FIVE: Beyond coping strategies **87**
Chapter 12: Thriving when the going is tough 89
Chapter 13: Taking time off work 93
Chapter 14: Returning to work 95

Part SIX: People's stories **97**
Chapter 15: Thoughts in the head are actually made up – Shelly's story 99
Chapter 16: A shift will take place – Jane's story 107
Chapter 17: Sense of empowerment – Mike's story 115
Chapter 18: Switching off from work mode – Hannah's story 121
Chapter 19: No longer responsible for other's actions – Samaira's story 127
Chapter 20: Feeling low is no longer a scary place – Phil's story 131

FINAL THOUGHTS 135
RESOURCES 141

Acknowledgements 143
About the Author 145

INTRODUCTION

Personal note from the author

A few years ago, during a personal coaching session, I complained to my coach that I had too much on my plate. I told her that I was overwhelmed by the endless jobs I had on my to-do list. I wanted her to understand how stressed I was feeling. I listed out my challenges, all of which were entirely convincing, I thought:

- I was working in a demanding job as a psychiatrist.
- I was a mother with two young kids.
- I didn't have outside help at home and no close family nearby.
- And, I was trying to set up my own coaching business and struggling to find the time for it.

I went on describing my problems in some detail, to convince my coach that anyone else in my shoes would have been as stressed and overwhelmed too. I have to admit; I was expecting strategies to stay calm and focused all of the time (or at least most of the time) and feel good in myself.

She responded in a gentle voice: 'I can't say you don't have a lot on your plate. You obviously do. You can only do so much.' I waited patiently to hear more.

'However, you do a lot of thinking about what you need to do, too, perhaps in excess? What if this was the source of your stress and not the actual work itself?'

I didn't like the sound of that.

I didn't want to hear what she'd said because she implied that I was creating my stress by overthinking. And, I didn't get any strategies to help me think any less. Instead, she went on to share the power of thought and its role in creating our experiences of reality.

We spent a couple of hours together. During the session, out of nowhere, something profound occurred to me. I can only describe that as an insight (a deep realisation) about what is true, for not just you and me but every human being on this planet.

It suddenly hit me that every person had access to innate health and resilience, that I had been looking at *fixing* people as a psychiatrist and focusing on their weaknesses most of the time. I had never seen it so clearly before, and I burst into tears!

That initial insight has gradually but fundamentally transformed the way I make sense of myself and the world around me. It has changed the way I practice as a psychiatrist and mental health coach.

I came out of the session feeling quite dazed but profoundly relieved. Although, I was somewhat disappointed that I didn't learn any mental strategies, at another level I knew that I'd stumbled across something quite fundamental and profound.

Since then, my understanding of innate health, resilience and the nature of thought has grown incrementally. This understanding has positively impacted different areas of my life. I can feel in touch with a deeper sense of peace and contentment like never before.

Have I ever felt stressed and anxious at work since? I sure have. But, understanding where my feelings of stress and anxiety came from, and my innate ability to bounce back from setbacks has helped me immensely.

What I'll be sharing in this book is not 'positive psychology'. I'll not ask you to think positive thoughts or reframe your negative work experiences to positive ones. I won't teach you step-by-step techniques nor give you tools and strategies to deal with work-related issues. I won't even ask you to analyse all the reasons you've felt stressed and anxious in your workplace.

Not for a moment am I denying that there are challenges to be dealt with, issues that need resolving. Step-by-step strategies, tools, and techniques may seem to help from time to time. However, you may have found that every time you solve one problem, a new one soon arises. It may seem like we're fighting a never-ending battle as overwhelming feelings of stress and anxiety keep resurfacing.

All too often, people seem to accept stress and anxiety as unavoidable consequences of the career they'd chosen. They continue to the day when prolonged stress manifests in the form of health issues – physical or psychological.

Back in November 2016, I decided to leave my full-time NHS consultant job in England. That wasn't because I was stressed out or experiencing burnout. Yes, my job was busy and demanding, and there were a few challenges at work. It seemed for a while that *those problems* caused my upset feelings. Luckily, I soon realised that just because it appeared that way didn't mean it was true. As my thinking changed, my experience changed.

My decision to leave was driven by a strong desire to be of service to more people. I was moved to share the understanding of *the principles of innate health and resilience* to a wider audience. It dawned on me that a lot of psychological pain and suffering can be alleviated by understanding how the mind works, and by having a deeper understanding of the inner resilience in all of us.

This book is a brief introduction to what I like to call the understanding of innate health and resilience, in the context of stress and anxiety in the workplace. This understanding is widely known as the *Three Principles* as articulated by the late Sydney Banks. Mr Banks was a Scottish welder who lived in British Columbia, Canada. He was by no means a highly educated person or an expert in the field of psychology or psychiatry. From what I understand, Mr Banks didn't even complete his formal high school education. However, following a series of insights and an enlightenment experience, whereby he had the most profound understanding of how the mind works, he changed overnight from an insecure to an enlightened human being. Everyone who knew him was baffled by this drastic change. People soon began flocking to him from far and wide. He started sharing his insights about the basic truths behind our psychological experiences of life. He pointed to three universal principles – mind, thought and consciousness (I've listed several good websites and books in the final chapter of this book, and I'd encourage you to find out more about the Three Principles and Mr Banks' work).

In the beginning, when I had shared the Three Principles or 3Ps, I got mixed reactions from people. They would ask: 'So, what are these Three Principles?' I'd find myself trying to define what I thought it meant. And, as I struggled to find the words to explain a formless, spiritual intelligence which is the source of all human experiences, people got confused. They'd start intellectualising about this understanding and begin to compare it with what they already knew or had come across before. Sadly, most of them didn't get curious enough, especially as there was no established evidence-base for this understanding. And, many were looking for approaches they could easily apply, and when they realised that the *Three Principles* wasn't a therapeutic tool as such, they weren't keen to explore any further.

Please note: *This book addresses the layperson in the modern workplace. I've kept the writing style as conversational and informal as possible (the way I understand information best). It isn't a guide to learning about the Three Principles in depth or as originally taught by Sydney Banks. Excellent resources in the form of books and videos by prominent authors are already available for the reader to explore (in the* Resources *section of the book).*

Unlike many experienced Three Principles educators who feel at ease to share the 3Ps understanding, I like sharing about innate health and resilience. I'm still pointing to the same fundamental truth behind all human experience, only using words I resonate with deeply as I continue my journey of extending my understanding.

Although, as I've mentioned above, one can't apply the Principles as a strategy to deal with stress and anxiety, there are implications to realising the true source of stress and anxiety and our psychological default system.

My hope is you, as a reader, will take this opportunity to explore an understanding that has helped many discover the illusionary nature of their thought-created realities. In doing so, I sincerely hope that you'll not only be able to turn stress on its head and understand the true nature of stress in the workplace but also discover something deeper and meaningful about life itself!

With loving wishes,

Rani
Devon, United Kingdom

What this book is about

This book is for you if you'd like to:

- Understand why sometimes you get stressed at work and not always (despite being in the same job routine)
- Feel relaxed and get productive at the same time
- Feel good feelings at work
- Learn about your invisible power – of innate health and resilience
- Understand why others around you (colleagues, boss, and customers) behave the way they sometimes do, and learn not take it personally

Why should you care to learn this

Too many people are stressed and anxious these days. Staff burnout from stress is a well-recognised problem, and stress is one of the leading causes of health problems in the workplace. The *Health and Safety Executive (HSE)* has defined stress as:

'The reaction people have to excessive demands or pressures, arising when people try to cope with tasks, responsibilities or other types of pressure connected with their job, but find difficulty, strain or worry in doing so.'

Several studies have shown the negative impact of stress and burnout on individuals and organisations as a whole. No one is immune from experiencing stress and anxiety.

According to a recent BBC report[1], the number of NHS[2] mental health staff who have had to take sick leave because of their mental health issues has risen

---

[1] BBC News, 22 September 2017:
http://www.bbc.co.uk/news/health-41172805

[2] NHS (National Health Service) is the public healthcare system of England, Scotland, Wales and Northern Ireland.

by 22% in the past five years. According to the HSE, over 11 million days are lost at work a year because of stress at work.

This book attempts to convey a message of hope.

Everyone has an innate capacity to bounce back from setbacks, reconnect with their passion for work, do their best and thrive no matter how dire external circumstances may seem.

As I've said earlier, this is not a book that promises to teach you strategies to tackle stress and anxiety in the workplace. In other words, it's not prescriptive, but descriptive and educational.

The humble aim of the book is to introduce and guide you to the path of deeper realisation and understanding of your experience of life. It will introduce you to your innate capacity to have fresh thoughts and a range of human emotions.

You'll hopefully also experience compassion for yourself and people in your life when you understand that everyone *experiences* life the same way as you.

All the individual stories depicted in the book are true stories of professionals currently working either in the public or private sector. The names have been changed to maintain confidentiality.

There are <u>three salient points</u> covered in this book:

1. We all have access to the gift of thought, the capacity for fresh thoughts and the ability to thrive.
2. All of our experiences (including feelings of stress and anxiety) come from the power of thought taking form in the moment, one hundred percent of the time.
3. The reality we experience is subjective, and each of us live in a *separate* reality. However, the mind is designed to work the same way all the time, in each of us.

❖ ❖ ❖

A <u>few distinctions</u> and words of caution –

Firstly, stress and anxiety are generated internally and can't be *caused* by anything external to us.

When I looked up the definition of stress in the dictionary, a couple of definitions caught my attention –

a) distress caused by having too many problems or too much to do.
b) A state of mental or emotional strain or tension resulting from adverse or demanding circumstances.

Both of these definitions imply that the cause of stress is external, that we feel stress because of something outside of us. These don't take into consideration the role of thought.

Recently, I came across a definition of stress by George Pransky (psychologist and Three Principles educator), which is unique, unconventional and perhaps controversial:

'Stress is nothing more than the weight of negative thinking taken seriously over time.'

Negative thoughts, such as worry, resentment, fear, and guilt, can turn on the *stress response* in the body – activating the hypothalamic-pituitary-adrenal (HPA) axis. The axis is meant to supply us with the chemical fuel we need (cortisol, adrenaline, noradrenaline, glucose) in our bloodstream to fight off or escape from real danger. Our ancestors needed it when they faced mortal danger in the course of their daily lives.

Over the years, we humans have learned to misuse and activate the same system by taking our negative thoughts too seriously, by worrying and ruminating about events or circumstances that are not life-threatening (quite unlike what our early ancestors may have experienced).

By innocently misusing the gift of thought, we create what Dr Bill Pettit (a U.S. psychiatrist and Three Principles educator) refers to as *a biochemical mess in our brain*, and there are implications, both in the short and the long term.

The point I wish to make is –

The common definitions of stress imply that the source of stress is *out there*. If that's the case, to manage our stress, we'd need to fix what's external to us. And if we can't, we would need to change our attitude, behaviour or learn to *control* our stress and anxiety by using whatever tools and means are available to us.

What if our beliefs about stress and the *common* understanding about how best to deal with stress aren't true?

It's time to turn the commonly held understanding about stress on its head!

The source of stress and anxiety is internal. We also make acute stress chronic (i.e. long-term) by innocently misusing the power of thought and spend hours indulging or trying to *fix* our negative thinking.

We're so used to doing something with our thinking that doing nothing seems counterintuitive and unhealthy. But, is it?

The second distinction being – unlike traditional self-help approaches to well-being, this understanding reminds us that we don't need to work on *not feeling stressed*, nor do we need to try to control our thoughts. All we need to do is sit back, and allow the mind to settle and quieten down on its own.

How do we do that?

We leave the content of our thinking alone as best as we can. A quiet mind is our default state of mind when we aren't paying attention to and taking our turbulent thoughts seriously.

Someone once said that we human beings are the only creatures who tend to go faster when we get lost. We do so by using the gift of thought against us. Other animals tend to stop or pause when they're lost and not being chased. If they get lost, they stop until they see where to go next. Perhaps, we need to do the same!

Once we realise the *inside-out nature* of our experiences, we'll see past the illusion painted by the mind that our source of stress and anxiety is *out there* somewhere.

A few words of caution...

CAUTION #1. As I've already mentioned a couple of times, what I'm sharing here is neither a tool nor technique. It's purely educational, and learning happens via insight (sight/realisation from within) rather than having an intellectual grasp of the understanding. This understanding is also not a substitute for someone needing to seek medical or psychiatric help.

CAUTION #2. It's normal to confuse the term *thought* for the act of thinking. What I am referring to here is an invisible power called thought that we have access to and from which we weave our *personal thoughts*. You can describe it as the source of energy from which we create the content of our thinking. More on this later.

CAUTION #3. The word *resilience* has become a buzz word. It seems like we need to do something or be a certain way to come across as resilient. It's also believed that some people have more resilience than others and that we can equip ourselves with tools to become more resilient. Resilience doesn't mean enduring immense pressure or hardship and marching on at the cost of physical and psychological exhaustion. That could put us and others at risk.

CAUTION #4. The so-called *simple truth* isn't a tool or strategy but an understanding or realisation about the nature of our experiences. Hence, some of the themes may seem repetitive – that's entirely deliberate to impress upon you the simplicity of the core message in this book.

What I am alluding to in this book is an innate and pre-existing intelligence. Every human being on earth has a natural capacity to think fresh, new thoughts and has access to an invisible power or energy. You don't have to do something unique to feel resilient. You already are a resilient being at your core.

At a fundamental level, you can tap into the space of resilience (or pre-existing intelligence) and feel resourceful. You will feel empowered to make decisions, take spontaneous action and live a fulfilled life – all at the same time.

Part ONE

Stress and Anxiety

1

Is the real source of our stressful and anxious feelings 'out there'?

Let's consider some factors that seem to bring stress and anxiety to the workplace - having a highly demanding job, needing to meet targets and deadlines, difficult colleagues, higher management, workplace politics, dwindling resources and so on. Feel free to add to the list.

Do any or all of the above cause stress and anxiety? Yes, it seems that way, doesn't it?

Despite all the challenges mentioned above, there are times when we're in a flow state, and we surprise ourselves. We're able to handle any challenge that comes our way. We usually feel good when that happens.

There'll be other days when we feel overwhelmed with stress and anxiety and struggle to connect to that previous 'flow state'. We then feel annoyed about it.

Same work pressure, same workplace, same colleagues, same usual office politics, same dwindling resources – and yet, we've different experiences at different times.

The explanations we come up with are like: 'I felt good because…'

- Things went according to plan.
- My colleagues understood me.
- The senior management highly praised us.

On the flip side, the other explanations may be: 'I felt stressed and anxious because…'

- Things didn't go according to plan.
- My colleagues disagreed with me.
- The senior management failed to recognise all the hard work we'd put into this project.

It may seem that things outside of us, in the workplace, have the power to make us feel a certain way.

It's as if there are a lot of *stress germs* (a term I first heard from Michael Neill, best-selling author, and transformative coach) in the workplace that is contagious. It can potentially get passed from one person to another. These *germs* seem to be more around work environments than say near beautiful holiday destinations (unless you live or work there!).

Of course, we all know that stress germs don't exist. However, it does seem like work environments, people at work and the job itself have the power to make us feel stressed.

Sure, there are times when we realise that stressful feelings have something to do with our stressful thoughts. But, most of us believe that our stressful thoughts are the by-product of what's happening *out there* or what could/would occur in the future.

It's so easy for us to point the finger at external reasons as the source of stress. Then, we either come up with solutions or find additional reasons for feeling stressed and anxious: we fall into the *'I'll be _____ if _____'* trap.

<u>I'll be happy and satisfied at work if</u>:

- I'm given a lot of support.
- People understand me and treat me with respect.
- People listen to me, and to my ideas.
- My boss is kind to me.
- People agree with me.
- I don't have too much to do.
- Things go smoothly at work.
- There are enough resources available.
- Everyone else around me works efficiently.

<u>I'll be stressed and anxious at work if</u>:

- I'm asked to deal with urgent work or manage a crisis.
- I've strict deadlines.
- There's a disagreement with my manager.
- I'm not acknowledged for all my hard work.
- I have to cover when others are off-sick.
- A customer behaves rudely with me.
- We're not meeting our sales targets.

In both instances above, it looks as if external situations keep us happy but can also be responsible for our stress and anxiety at work.

Either way, it seems like we're at the mercy of our environment and external factors over which we've little or no control.

It then feels, that unless our external circumstances improve, we will continue to feel stressed and anxious. The stories of the following individuals illustrate that experience -

Phil[3] works as a surgeon within the NHS. He had suffered stress and burnout about three years ago and was on the verge of taking sick leave. At that time, Phil believed that the healthcare system had to change before he could work efficiently and enjoy his work. He blamed the healthcare system for feeling stressed at work.

Mike[4] who also works in the NHS as a counsellor, had to take time off work due to stress. He struggled to see eye to eye with his manager and felt that the management team cared less for staff and patients and more about reaching monthly targets. He thought that his feelings of stress and overwhelm came from the pressure of more performance targets each month.

---

[3] Read Phil's full story in chapter 20
[4] Read Mike's full story in chapter 17

2

What's the True Source of Stress and Anxiety in the workplace?

A better question might be – 'Where does our <u>experience of stress and anxiety in the workplace stem from?</u>' If it truly comes from our work circumstances or colleagues, why do our experiences wax and wane despite little changes in our outside world? We can have a myriad of experiences in any given day, despite what goes on at work.

Jane[5] works as a ward manager in an acute psychiatric inpatient unit. She has multiple roles, ranging from delivering a safe, recovery-oriented service and implementing change to managing and motivating staff. She used to struggle at business meetings, especially when she felt that people

_____

[5] Read Jane's story in chapter 16

weren't agreeing with her or they didn't seem to understand her points of view.

It seemed to her that her feelings of anxiety and defensiveness were because of people behaving a certain way. She didn't experience the same level of discomfort all the time though. It was hard for her to see that her experiences of anxiety and defensiveness were generated internally via thought in the moment.

<u>Why does our experience of stress and anxiety seem to wax and wane?</u>

There is only one explanation: *The mind works only one way. We can only experience thought taking form at any moment in time, from moment to moment.* And, the nature of thought is such that it's ever-changing. One moment we can have a *good* thought and feel good. The next moment we can have a *rubbish* thought and feel bad.

That explains why our experiences of stress and anxiety always vary. Some days, we feel extremely stressed and maybe convinced that the only answer is to quit your job. Other days, we remember why we love our job and feel grateful that we get to serve others.

As the form of thought changes, our experiences seem to change.

Yes, our experiences feel real but they aren't coming directly from what's happening *out there*. Our experiences are generated internally one hundred percent of the time. It comes from thought in the moment.

Mara Gleason, author of *One Thought Changes Everything* describes the working of the mind beautifully –

'...Many people assume we are like cameras, walking around taking snapshots of the world out there. Whatever is there, our *camera* is objectively capturing it. But in truth, the mind works more like an old-fashioned film projector. From the human mind, via thought, we create a picture of life and project it out onto the screen of our experience. We live in a movie of our own making. Mind is the power source, thought is the film, and consciousness is the bulb that lightens it up.'

3

Where do Feelings come from?

The only way we can experience our work, colleagues or work circumstances is via thought in the moment. It works the same way with every single experience we have. But for the sake of this book and subject matter, let's focus on issues that we face at work.

I don't want you to take anything I say for granted. I invite you to see what resonates with you when your mind is quiet and still. What I'm sharing might seem very strange, perhaps even impossible at first. But, please bear with me.

No one likes to suffer, and yet we all encounter different kinds of suffering during our lives. We innocently create a lot of pain and suffering that looks and feels very real to us.

The pain is real to us.

The suffering is real <u>to us</u>.

And yet, all the intense, uncomfortable feelings aren't caused directly by our problems or circumstances. Feelings are generated internally via the power of thought taking form (or shape) in the moment. Anytime thought takes form we usually feel it (the *thought-feeling* connection).

Our intellect looks for the cause of our feelings outside of us, in our situation or circumstances. That's because we've learned to assume that things happening in the outside world cause us to feel a certain way.

Our formed thoughts and feelings are like two sides of the same coin.

We feel our thinking at any moment, not what's happening *out there*.

An association between work issues and feelings of stress and anxiety is widely recognised. However, such an association won't be misunderstood as <u>causation</u> once we understand that all our experiences are the product of thought at any given time.

Let's suppose your workload had the power to make you feel stressed and overwhelmed to any extent. If that was true, the amount of stress and overwhelm you feel should always be directly proportional to the amount of your workload. Also, we'd then expect all of your colleagues doing a similar job to experience the same level of distress too. But, that's not what we see from studies of work-related stress.

The levels of stress and anxiety we all experience vary from day to day, moment to moment and isn't the same for all working within the same organisational environment.

Some will admit that circumstances do not always cause feelings. They realise that they *overthink* and become preoccupied with work-related issues. They understand that their thinking about work causes them stress.

But, here's the distinction – they see thinking as an <u>effect of the fact</u> – they will argue their point that their job was stressful and had *caused* the experience of stress and anxiety in the first place.

Rationally and intellectually, that may seem true. But, it truly isn't.

I didn't know that my job and personal circumstances weren't the true sources of my experience of stress in the past. As I'd mentioned in the beginning, when my coach gently pointed me to the connection between thought and feeling of stress, I could see that I worried excessively about my workload and jobs that were unfinished.

However, I honestly believed that if I hadn't had too much to do, I wouldn't have felt stressed in the first place. I could accept that there were times I brought on my feelings of stress by overthinking. But, at other times I was convinced that my experience of stress was coming from *out there* – from my job and other events in my life.

It's funny looking back at that coaching session; I chuckle at how self-righteous I was and how desperately I wanted to convince my coach that I was right!

How can our circumstances cause us to have a certain experience? Well, they can't.

Our stressful feelings (or experiences), or any feelings for that matter, aren't caused by our circumstances, our past or other people. Our stressful feelings or any feelings for that matter are shadows of formed thoughts. In other words, emotions are inseparable from thought taking form at that moment.

Another way of emphasising the thought-feeling connection is this – *If we are feeling something, we are feeling thought in the moment.* We may or may not be aware of this at all.

Simply put – we may not be aware of thoughts going on in the background. We may only feel them.

According to this understanding of innate health and resilience, we can only experience the invisible and infinite power of thought taking form from moment to moment.

The intellect then looks outside in a quest to decipher the feeling. It uses the five senses to make sense of the world around it. It gives meaning to our experiences of events, circumstances, places, and people. Our intellect **creates our thinking** about where our feelings are coming from.

Without the power of thought, we can't have an experience. It's as fundamental to our life experience as air to our breathing.

Shelly[6] is a registered general nurse (RGN) and works in the NHS. She moved up the ranks and became a senior manager very early on in her career. Before coming across the principles of innate health and resilience, Shelly had experienced stress and burnout after taking on a higher management role in a new service. Her job was very busy, and she was regularly working long hours.

She had to take time off work for about four months. After returning, she struggled to get on with her colleagues and other job issues, despite reducing some of her responsibilities. Three years later, she found her mental health deteriorating again and noticed the signs and symptoms of stress and burnout returning.

At one point Shelly was struggling to such an extent that she had to take diazepam on a regular basis to calm her nerves and turn up at work. Her doctor diagnosed her with *clinical depression*.

---

[6] Read Shelly's full story in chapter 15

One of her first insights as a result of coming to this understanding of innate health was that the thoughts (personal thinking) in her head were made up (from the power of thought). Realising that helped her immensely. She still has the occasional bad day or moments when she gets caught up in her thinking. However, she has never felt so healthy in years.

Just like Shelly, I've been fortunate to come to see the truth of this. I continue to get tricked into believing that my experiences (both good and bad) come from my circumstances.

After all, thought does appear convincingly real!

It soon dawns on me that I can only ever have an experience via thought in the moment and that my experience will change when my thinking changes by itself. It frees me up from needless pain and suffering, allowing me instead to get on with life and live life as best as I can.

4

Why what we Think Appears Real

Our brain has what my Three Principles mentor and friend, Dr Bill Pettit, calls a *special effects department.* As the power of thought takes form, moment to moment, thought changes from the impersonal (formless) to the personal (form). Metaphorically speaking, the special effects department in the brain continuously uses the energy of thought (formless energy) to create instant, unique physical effects or form (via a complex burst of neuronal activities and chemical processes), thereby generating powerful feelings in the body.

When we're feeling acutely stressed and anxious, we activate the sympathetic nervous system which results in a cascade of neurochemical activities. We get into what is commonly known as the *fight-flight-freeze* mode.

In other words, we experience the stress in our entire physiology, and the experience is indeed authentic to us.

We ask ourselves: 'Why am I feeling stressed?' The intellect comes up with answers that seem very plausible to us.

'I'm feeling stressed because I've so much to do and I might not make the noon deadline' or, 'If only my boss was kind and understanding, I wouldn't be feeling stressed about my job right now.'

We don't realise that the experience of stress is brought to life by a thought taking form in the moment and further amplified by the intellect attaching a particular meaning to the experience, thereby creating more thoughts!

Samaira[7] is a design consultant and works in a design firm. A significant part of her role is to achieve sales targets on a regular basis. In the past, she used to feel stressed and overwhelmed, thinking she had to take responsibility for other people's actions, including their poor performance at work. Her thinking looked real to her. Since learning about

---

[7] Read Samaira's story in chapter 19

how the mind works, she gets it that: 'I am not responsible for others' actions.'

It's important to realise that it's not what we think that matters, but **that we think**.

Imagine that your thoughts are like transient energy bubbles. From the infinite source of power of thought, energetic thought bubbles keep popping up all the time. Our awareness (i.e. consciousness) shines a light on some of these bubbles and brings them to life with the help of the *special effects* department in the brain, making them real.

We can feel those energetic thought bubbles in the whole body. That's the reason why when we're in the midst of a thought-storm[8], it's almost impossible to talk ourselves out of it. It forms our reality, and that personal reality seems like the truth.

When we're in it, we're in it!

---

[8] I define *thought-storm* as a sudden, turbulent state of mind when we've too many thoughts swirling around cluttering our head space. These thoughts seem so powerful and so real that identifying them as an illusion of mind is next to impossible.

The more we try to talk ourselves out of a thought storm, more and more energetic thought bubbles cluster together, and we drown in our negative experience. It's hard to escape falling for the movie plot with special effects. It seems vividly real.

But, as thoughts are transient bubbles of energy soon the thought storm moves away, giving way to new thoughts.

People sometimes disagree and say they feel stressed even when they're not thinking about their problems. They argue that circumstances make them feel a certain way, which then leads to thoughts that further intensify the feelings.

I used to believe that too. It was hard to get my head around it when I first came across the principles of innate health and resilience. My understanding at the time was — thought created feelings and feelings created thought too. It seemed to me that thought equalled content of my thinking. I had no awareness of the source from which thoughts took form. I had assumed our thoughts were simply activities that arose from the brain. I also assumed that mind was simply a part of the brain (that's a story for another time).

Looking back, I realise my innocence in falling for the illusion that somehow the external world had the power to make me and others think or feel a certain way. It seemed that we'd feel and think good thoughts if our external world was favourable and not otherwise.

Here's how I see it now.

What we refer to as external stimuli or the external world, has no power whatsoever to make us feel or think in a certain way. It's just a convincing illusion that we keep falling for again and again.

Our experiences will always seem like the ultimate reality. In other words, our thinking will always appear real to us – until we *see* that it's not true!

Part TWO

The Self-correcting System

5

Our Psychological Immune System

*"We are only ever one thought
away from happiness, or one thought
away from sadness."*

– SYDNEY BANKS

'Let's wait for a shift (to happen),' Jane, the mental health ward manager I introduced earlier, shares her understanding that transformations occur, and a person acutely unwell or distressed gradually calms down and does get better. It's important to note here that sometimes when people are acutely unwell or experiencing extreme emotional turmoil, use of appropriate tools such as medication treatment can help with symptom relief.

Jane is now able to see beyond a person's acute and immediate presentation and recognises the health and resilience at their core. That doesn't mean she no longer needs to offer support to her patients, but her actions now come from a place of knowing and a better understanding.

So, how does a shift happen?

Simply put, anytime our thinking changes, effortlessly and naturally, our feelings change. Change occurs when our mind gets quiet, and we start to access fresh thoughts.

So, what is our default psychological immune system?

We all have an awareness of our body's immune system. Unless we have a problem with our immune system, we know that any cut or wound usually will heal with time.

If the wounds are superficial, they usually heal fast, and if they are intense, it might take a while. We may need to have a specific treatment, but eventually, the wound is expected to heal. We know that we can't speed up the healing process by poking and disturbing the wound – it will heal at its own pace. The less we interfere, the better.

What if we had a similar psychological immune system that heals psychological wounds? Unlike our physical injuries that we can see, our psychological wounds aren't visible. They can only be experienced and can be equally (and sometimes more) distressing.

Our psychological wounds can manifest in the form of mental, emotional and physical health issues, and sometimes even as *medically-unexplained symptoms*. Unknown to most of us, our psychological immune system is quietly working away in the background, healing our psychological wounds, clearing old thoughts and making space for new ones.

If we fail to notice that we have a psychological immune system, we'll always feel that it was down to us to figure out ways to *fix* our distressed mental states. By doing so, we'll innocently keep getting in the way of the spontaneous healing of the mind.

How do we get in the way?

Using the analogy of physical wound healing, analysing what happened and revisiting the past repeatedly to help us heal our psychological wounds is like poking continuously at our emotional wounds expecting to speed up the process of healing.

When someone experiences stress and anxiety related to the workplace, usually they end up discussing their situation with other people. They get into analysing what went wrong and why. Unknown to them, the more they *investigate* their problems, the longer it takes for them to get new insights and make progress.

Mike used to do just that. He and his team used to stress and complained a lot about various challenges at work. He confided that engaging in those conversations in the past fuelled more thoughts, and feelings of anger and frustration.

It's helpful to see that the experiences of stress and anxiety are fleeting because thought in the moment is fleeting and keeps changing. The more we analyse our thinking, the more we get in the way of our innate psychological wound healing.

Psychological well-being and resilience are innate. We have access to an infinite source of well-being and resilience at our core. That has nothing to do with our intellect or external circumstances.

Most people don't realise this. We seem to have lost access to our innate health and resilience by our attention to depressed mood, stressful thinking and *innocent misuse* of the gift of thought.

The good news is that even when we seem to lose access to our innate health and resilience, it's still there. It's only *hidden from view.* As our mind gets still, we get glimpses of what's already there, within us.

'Hang on a minute,' you might say, 'If I don't deal with the things that seem to cause my stress and anxiety, things could go from bad to worse, and I might have a complete meltdown. Surely, I shouldn't let that happen, right?'

You'll need to address that and make adjustments in your life, in a way that makes sense to you.

For example, if you're working longer hours, are unable to get enough rest and feeling exhausted, that potentially will have an adverse impact on your physical and psychological well-being.

You may need to highlight that with your manager to get the help and support you need. You will perhaps need to make changes to your lifestyle, ensure you eat a healthy balanced diet, exercise and maintain a good sleep routine. You'll need to use your common sense and take all practical steps necessary to look after yourself.

Similarly, if there are issues in the workplace that need to be addressed by someone else, you'll want to look at resolving that with the appropriate person or management as best as you can.

It's important to know that there's a big difference between dealing with an issue at a practical level and addressing the issue by overthinking and repeated analysing.

Hence, the main point I want to emphasise is this:

There are no issues *out there* as such. An *issue* is again made up via thought. Our consciousness, with the aid of the **special effects** part of our brain, brings alive our thoughts and makes those very compelling and real.

As you begin to see that your experience of an issue in the workplace is thought generated, you also start to see that – as your thoughts change your experiences change. You can have a fresh perspective about work and an entirely new experience at any given moment.

Everyone, including you, has an innate capacity to access fresh thoughts and new insights.

The issue for Jane was that people either didn't seem to understand her views or they were defensive about certain changes she wanted to introduce.

Once she had fresh insights into the nature of her experience and understood that people were perhaps reacting from a place of fear, it ceased to be so much of a problem. She was able to stop taking people's reactions personally and managed to listen and communicate more efficiently.

All of us have the innate capacity to -

- Recover, grow and progress.
- Think fresh thoughts no matter how long we have been focusing on old, negative thoughts.

6

The Nature of Thought

Thought is to thinking what air is to breathing (and we think and breathe naturally).

Just like we breathe, we think. From the moment we're born to the moment we die, we'll breathe, and we'll think. Both these processes happen on their own, automatically and naturally.

We don't have to teach a baby how to breathe when it emerges from the womb. It seems to know what to do. We don't need to teach a growing baby or toddler to think thoughts. They appear to do it naturally.

I haven't come across anyone who'd disagree with the fact that we breathe and we think. What's the evidence that we do both? Well, we experience it first-hand.

Sure, we can learn how to take deep breaths, and we also learn how to think a certain way or what thoughts to give our attention. But, even if we don't try to make it happen, we naturally breathe in and out, and we naturally have access to the power to weave thoughts.

Now, we all know we think, and at times we overthink.

But, we may not have realised that we have access to a power which allows us to have an experience of life. We also use this power to weave thoughts.

And, thoughts are ever-changing. Thoughts form, come to our awareness, and then they go off. One thought comes to our attention and dissipates, and another thought comes along.

Sometimes, we have fewer thoughts in our mind and are in a *flow* state. At other times, we feel overwhelmed by too many thoughts and happen to be in a *stuck* state.

A clear mind is our natural, default state. When we allow ourselves to have any experience (any feelings), we're in a flow state.

Anytime we judge our experiences or make it wrong, our mind gets cluttered, and we feel stressed.

Anytime we don't take our thoughts or feelings seriously, we seem to get back into a flow state with ease. And, we relax.

As the form of thought changes, our experiences change.

What if the power which helps us experience life and with which we weave our personal thoughts is pure, spiritual energy or *life-force* energy?

What if this energy is pre-existing intelligence, neutral (neither good nor bad) and impersonal?

What if any experience we have – using this power – is okay at a deeper, spiritual level?

Sydney Banks once said: *'If the only thing people learned was not to be afraid of their experience, that alone would change the world.'*

Prior to coming across the principles behind innate health and resilience, I used to be fearful of my negative experiences. I relied heavily on tools and techniques to fix my feelings.

I practised what I knew best at the time – to try and hold onto positive emotions (by using visualisation, positive affirmations, thinking happy thoughts, keeping a gratitude journal, tapping on acupressure points and so on). I tried hard to get rid of negative ones (using emotional freedom techniques or EFT, talking to my husband or others close to me, replacing negative thoughts with positive thoughts and so on).

After all, I was a psychiatrist and a well-being coach, and I couldn't afford to get anxious, upset, angry or frustrated. I couldn't afford to say: 'I'm only human.' At least, that's what I thought!

Sometimes, some of those strategies I applied seemed to help, but not always. One thing I can say with certainty - all of the techniques seemed to work some of the time, but none of them worked all of the time. Noticeably, they wouldn't work when I needed them most – when I was in the midst of a *thought-storm!*

It was no wonder that I kept looking for more and more tools to add to my *therapeutic toolbox.* I had learned about deep-seated (often unconscious) limiting beliefs during my coaching and psychotherapy training (as a trainee psychiatrist).

And so, when the techniques I employed to fix a negative feeling didn't work, I assumed I had unconscious limiting beliefs that were getting in the way of the techniques working. I assumed I needed to do more work on myself!

I didn't see my personal thoughts as transient and had no idea about the role of thought in generating my experiences from moment to moment.

❖ ❖ ❖

Thoughts aren't real but appear very real. The more strongly we believe them, analyse them, indulge them, the more stressed we feel.

The less we entertain our stressful or negative thoughts and see beyond the illusionary nature of our thought-generated reality, the more we get in touch with our innate health and resilience.

Mike is now aware that his negative experiences of the workplace aren't generated by the managers, by the system or other factors in the workplace but by his thinking about those.

He realises something he hadn't realised before – that he had a choice. 'I can choose to get caught up in all that, but it makes me more stressed and bitter. Or, I can carry on doing the best I can. Knowing this gives me a sense of empowerment – it's incredibly empowering.'

He goes on to say: 'I have my moments, but I know that's just my human experience. I often tell myself, "You don't have to believe your thinking," and I smile at myself because I genuinely believe that now.'

7

Implications of understanding innate psychological health and resilience

"You don't need to put the yolk in the egg. The yolk is already in the egg."
- VALDA MONROE

As our thoughts change, so do our feelings and physiology. We don't need to get rid of the stressful thoughts or think positive thoughts. That only adds to the clutter in our head, and we feel overwhelmed.

All thoughts are neutral unless we attach meaning to them and judge them as right or wrong.

I'm not saying that we should or shouldn't judge our experiences. After all, we are lucky to have an intellect that helps us make moral judgements, make decisions, analyse facts and figures, understand and interpret data, and take action when needed.

I'm not implying that there're no challenges in the workplace, expectations from management and bosses, targets to meet, colleagues you may not get along with, scarce resources and so forth.

But the fact remains – the only way you can experience any of the above is via the power of thought taking form in the moment.

Why is this important to know?

a) You may fall for the illusion of being stressed and anxious because of what's happening outside of you. However, once you realise that your feelings come from thought in the moment and not from external circumstances, it'll free you up.

b) You'll be less compelled to act on your stressful thoughts that feel real and uncomfortable.

c) Once you understand the transient nature of thoughts, and that they're harmless, you won't feel frightened of your thoughts and feelings anymore.

    d) You'll become aware of the natural psychological health and resilience in you.

If you want to learn more about the implications of this understanding especially regarding work-related stress and anxiety, make sure you take the time to read the truly inspiring stories in Part Six of this book.

Part THREE

States of Mind

8

Bringing out the best in you

Have you ever wondered why you couldn't recall your last ten thoughts or even your last five thoughts?

Have you also ever wondered why you can't predict what specific thoughts will occur to you in the future, say in the next five or ten minutes?

Thoughts are flowing continuously and swiftly. You don't have to hold on to the *positive* thoughts or work on letting go of the *negative* ones. They come and go anyway.

In the past, I tried hard to bring out the best in me by changing the way I felt. I learned that positive thoughts are like Teflon (they slip by very fast) and negative ones are like Velcro (they stick around). I learned and used techniques to reverse that, i.e. to make my positive thoughts last longer and for the negative thoughts to disappear faster. As I've already discussed, those techniques didn't help much or for long. And, it was sheer hard work!

I still remember a passing comment my husband once made, certainly before either of us had come to this understanding. I must have reacted and behaved in an unpleasant way for him to say what he said.

Honestly, I can't recall the event, but he said as a matter of fact: 'I think all the things you keep doing to make yourself a better person aren't working.'

I went bright red. 'How dare he!' I thought to myself.

I mumbled something angrily and stormed out of the room, fuming. I felt very hurt.

However, I believed him! I was trying desperately to be a better version of myself in many respects – a better mother, wife and partner, a better coach and psychiatrist, a better team player at work, a better human being…

I was working so hard to be positive, optimistic, joyful, grateful, enthusiastic, loving, cheerful... and, I felt I was failing to live up to my expectations.

I used to think that there was something fundamentally wrong with me for getting upset, for feeling negative and emotionally *losing it* frequently. Little did I know that I was aiming to have superhuman powers!

I feel much freer after coming across this understanding.

I remember telling my husband that he was right about the observation he had made back then. It was impossible for me to become a better version of myself by using techniques to *manipulate* how I felt. I was simply getting caught up in my thinking as it happens to us when we feel insecure. I already had what I was looking for! There was fundamentally nothing wrong with me. It felt quite good to be able to say that to him. And, all he did was smile. He had come to realise it too.

Having this understanding of innate health makes me realise that I don't need to work on myself to be a better version of me. I don't need to use tools or techniques to change the way I think, feel and behave. And yet, interestingly, when I stop trying, the best in me seems to come out more often and at the same time I *lose it* less often.

So, how do you bring out the best in you?

How do you get to be in a **flow state**?

How do you quiet your mind?

You don't have to fight or resist the negative thoughts that come your way. You don't have to hold on to the positive thoughts that come your way. I've already mentioned why those strategies don't work.

No particular approach will ever bring out the best in you every time, all the time.

Here's what I'd suggest though –

- Don't take your thoughts seriously.
- Rather than paying attention to your personal thoughts and analysing them, start to be curious about the source of all thoughts, good and bad.

Could thought simply be a constant stream of energy and information?

The flow of thought never stops, not even when you're in a deep sleep (also known as slow-wave or non-rapid eye movement sleep). There is, of course, a difference in your experience in an awake and a sleep state.

When you're asleep, you *aren't* acting like the *thought police*. Thoughts take all kinds of shapes, they dance around for a while, and then they dissipate.

When you're fast asleep, your intellect (now sleeping too) can't control your thinking. And yet, your thinking in the form of dreams seem vividly real, as you can often experience the physical manifestation of your thoughts. When you wake up, you feel relieved that it was just a dream, especially if it was a frightening or negative one.

Similarly, when you're awake, you go about life with the energy of thought in the background flowing continuously.

The difference is, the *thought police* is on duty now – your intellect. It monitors your thoughts and tries to make sense of your experiences by relying on the five senses and old memory files in the brain.

When you recognise thought not simply as the content of your thinking, but as the power fuelling your thinking, and notice its role in creating your day-to-day experiences, your mind gets quieter. Your *thought police* goes off duty for a while and you feel more relaxed. You feel less stressed, despite what's going on in your environment or workplace. You function more from a settled and uncluttered mind.

Yes, the *thought police* can never be made redundant. It's needed and has a significant role. However, you'll soon find its rightful place in your life and learn to use it wisely.

Understanding innate health and resilience allows us to show up at work as a human being first. We get to bring our authentic self to work. Like Shelly says: 'I show up as I am. I don't have to put a mask on and go to work.' We can choose to be comfortable in our skin, with our strengths and weaknesses and fulfil our roles to the best of our abilities.

Like Jane, we begin to get better at noticing how easily we slip back into believing our thinking and permit ourselves to step back, in whatever way makes sense to us. Like her, we too can feel connected with our wisdom and common sense more often than not and become more efficient and productive in the workplace.

9

The space for reflection

*"The intuitive mind is a sacred gift,
and the rational mind is a faithful
servant. We have created a society
that honours the servant and has
forgotten the gift."*

— ALBERT EINSTEIN

Notice that you can generate any thought, anytime, even right now!

It could be as simple as thinking – 'huh! Really?' or, 'Why does this matter?'

It could be a helpful, pleasant or bizarre thought, neutral or dark thought. It could be any thought – you get to make it up.

I am pointing this out to illustrate the fact that our individual, personal thoughts are our creation using our intellect and the constant flow of universal energy called **thought**.

We also have a free will. If we want to, we could keep ruminating over the same old thoughts that have gone past their *use by* date. Thoughts such as: 'Why did this happen to me?' or, 'They should've listened to me' or, 'I shouldn't have behaved that way' are a few examples.

Notice also that even if you aren't consciously thinking about something, thoughts just seem to pop up from nowhere. You'll begin to realise that new ideas simply appear out of nowhere, sometimes when you're least expecting them.

Contrary to traditional advice about thinking positive or seeing the glass as half full rather than half empty, I'm not suggesting you choose positive thoughts over negative thoughts, or that you put conscious effort into creating fresh thinking. I hope you're beginning to see why.

Our behaviour is after the fact of thought taking form. If there is a feeling of *dis-ease*, we try to fix that feeling. If we don't understand the principles of innate health and resilience, we'll continue to believe the contents of our thinking and try to fix our feelings of stress and anxiety. We'll keep turning to others for guidance and advice rather than trusting our wisdom and common sense.

That is what Hannah[9], who works as a therapist in the NHS, felt she had to do in the past. Hannah has been working as a therapist in the NHS for over a decade in specialist mental health services. She used to doubt some of her decision-making. At work, she used to seek out her colleagues for reassurance. She'd go home and talk through her worries with her husband, again looking for reassurance that she was doing a good job at work.

And now, Hannah can trust her wisdom and common sense and is self-confident as a therapist. She's able to reflect on her practice and seek support when she needs it. Hannah doesn't feel the need to seek reassurance as she used to in the past. That means she's now able to switch off from work when she gets home, find mental stillness and enjoy quality time with her family.

We have an infinite capacity to think new thoughts and act from a higher level of consciousness than we believe possible.

---

[9] You can read Hannah's full story in chapter 18

If we don't understand the principles of innate health and resilience, we'll have no clue that the fresh and innovative ideas we seem to come up with from time to time can never be exhausted.

Take some time to reflect on the above and see if it makes sense to you.

❖❖❖

Your experiences in the workplace are bound to vary, changing from good to bad in the blink of an eye, as soon as an uncomfortable thought comes to your awareness.

Similarly, even if you've had a lot of bad experiences lately, your *experience* can change from bad to good in the blink of an eye. That's possible too. After all, as Sydney Banks used to say: *'We are only ever one thought away from happiness, or one thought away from sadness.'*

The more you realise the thought-feeling connection, that thoughts are transient, and they move on to be replaced by fresh ideas, the more psychologically healthy you'll feel.

No wonder Phil feels psychologically healthy despite working full-time as a surgeon, a job most would agree to be intellectually and physically very demanding.

Phil says: 'My emotions still go up and down. I still find myself in situations where I feel low. But, they're different in that it's no longer a scary place because I know it's temporary. And, I know from experience that unless I look for the cause of my feelings on the outside and try to repair the situation on the outside to fix the feeling, I know that my thoughts will flow and my feelings will flow with them. I find myself in a different place!'

10

Self-management or self-regulation are quick fixes at best

Emotions are seen as positive or negative. Examples of positive or healthy emotions are feelings of love, gratitude, joy, kindness, peace, contentment, and so forth.

Unhealthy or *negative* emotions are feelings of fear, worry, stress, anger, jealousy, hatred etc.

Most of us can accept the fact that we can't escape the so-called negative emotions from time to time. If we had a choice, we would choose to feel good rather than bad. When we feel negative, we want to *fix* that feeling and replace it with a positive one.

And as I've mentioned before, we look for tools and strategies – to manage and fix our negative feelings. Some of us also indulge in and gradually get hooked into problem habits such as – compulsive eating, getting into obsessional routines, procrastinating, consuming alcohol, using tranquilisers – all in our daily quest for a good feeling.

Many get motivated to exercise regularly, practice yoga, meditate, go for long walks, to not take on too much work, to cope with stress and anxiety.

However, all those habits and activities (some very desirable) tend not to work or be effective all the time.

So, what's going on?

If indulging in certain activities help, surely it should help every single time.

As I've already alluded to, there's something deeper at play. Our experiences ebb and flow. As our thinking changes on its own, our experience changes too.

I want to reiterate – I'm not for a moment suggesting that people should be in denial and not take any action.

Paying too much attention to thoughts takes us away from the present moment.

Paying less attention to thoughts declutters our mind and makes us more focused on the task at hand.

Phil, the surgeon, realises that the time and energy he can expend ruminating about problems in his workplace are invested better when he takes his concerns to appropriate forums within the organisation.

If self-management is not the answer, what is?

Self-awareness – Understanding that we create our experience of reality, that we have an innate capacity to access fresh thoughts, to recover from setbacks and that we all have a self-correcting psychological system.

Self-compassion – Seeing our innocence, that we keep falling for our *thought-created reality*. That, we always do our best at our level of awareness or state of mind.

<u>Should I not try to fix my stressful feelings?</u>

No, you don't need to fix the way you feel.

When you truly understand the nature of thought, that all feelings arise from thinking in the moment, and are not dangerous, at some point, it won't make any sense to attempt to fix your stressful feelings.

How can you ever fix something that isn't broken and is ever-changing!

I acknowledge that some people find using certain psychological or behavioural techniques or therapies helpful at times.

At best, most of these can be quick, symptomatic fixes and may seem to bring about relief temporarily. People then assume that they felt better because of using a particular strategy or therapy tool. In fact, any change that happens is because of a shift in their level of awareness, brought about by new thoughts coming their way.

Here's the catch though – At some level, a person will have to believe that a particular tool or therapy works or could work for them. If they don't have that belief, it's highly unlikely that they'll benefit from it.

Here's another problem – Inherent in using tools and strategies is the fact that the person would need to do something regularly to feel different. Once they stop that routine, the distressing feelings usually return, especially if their work circumstances or people around them haven't changed in that time.

That partly explains why people tend to get addicted to things outside of them in an attempt to feel better – illicit substances such as street drugs or legal highs, heavy alcohol consumption, gambling or even getting hooked on self-help techniques.

Why do we try to fix our feelings then?

There's a prevailing assumption that we shouldn't be feeling negative emotions. We assume that we should avoid unpleasant feelings such as anxiety, fear, frustration, anger and sadness as *they are wrong*.

It's important to remind ourselves that people are only trying to feel better, to fix their stressful feelings and doing the best they can, given their misunderstanding of the nature of thought, the thought-feeling connection and how the mind works.

Mike had spent years trying to change the way he felt. He believed that if he didn't change his thinking or manage his negative feelings, he'd suffer for the rest of his life. He had used food to cope with stress in the past and had developed an eating disorder.

Mike had two main coping strategies. The healthy strategy was running, and the unhealthy one led to an obsession about cleaning (he had suffered from an obsessive-compulsive disorder in the past). He felt immense relief when he finally realised that he didn't have to work so hard to fix his experiences. 'I can sit with my feelings much better,' he said, 'I know they'll pass, perhaps not as fast as I want them to but they'll pass. It's less hard work.'

Mike realised, so did all the others who've shared their stories in this book, that *to be human is to have all kinds of experiences, not just the pleasant but also the unpleasant ones.*

So, you can experience feelings of stress and anxiety in the workplace and know that you're still okay, that your experiences have nothing to do with your circumstances. Your experiences are coming from the power of thought taking form in the moment.

11

Dealing with 'difficult' people at work

"Bad behaviour is people acting out of insecurity, if we see this as wilful we tend to want to control and punish, but if we see this bad behaviour as people acting out of insecurity, then we tend to want to help them."
— JACK PRANSKY

'Difficult' people don't exist. However, people can act in ways that another person can label as being *difficult*.

All of us experience life the same way – from the inside out. All our experiences are generated internally via the power of thought taking form. And, every human being falls for the illusion that their experiences are caused by what's happening outside of them – it seems to us that our experiences have nothing or very little to do with thought-in-the-moment taking form.

Just like you, everyone else at work is walking around with their personal TCR (**thought-created reality**) experience, using the power of thought.

Using this power, they have views about themselves, others and the world around them. Just like our thinking may seem real to us, another person's thinking appears very real to them too. The same way we get lost in our little TCR world, they do too!

As we act out our stressful or insecure thinking sometimes, so do our colleagues and our bosses. When they're relaxed at work, their behaviour or attitude towards us and others may be entirely different.

Same person – different states of mind – different behaviour.

So, why is it useful to understand that we all experience life the same way (i.e. inside-out), but behave differently?

We can allow ourselves to step back when someone's acting unacceptably, e.g. being hostile or acting rude. We know that it's nothing to do with us and it's their *stuff*. They've been momentarily caught up in their thought-created reality bubble and are acting out of that reality.

When we realise that we're all the same, we feel compassion for others as well as for ourselves. We recognise that we're all doing the best we can, given the quality of thought and our level of understanding at any moment. We start to see what's common between us rather than what's different. We don't take other's beliefs, attitudes and behaviours personally.

As a senior manager, it has been beneficial for Shelly to see past people's bad behaviour to realise that they were acting out of insecurity. She soon understood and was able to reach out and help them.

We'll realise that it's not possible to see eye-to-eye with another person all the time and that we have different viewpoints and opinions. It doesn't mean that we're right and they're wrong or vice versa. It just means that their perception of reality is different from ours. Knowing that allows us to listen to them and have an open conversation.

As Shelly shares in her story, when she first returned to work from sick leave she struggled as she felt judged by her colleagues. She had a lot of judgemental thoughts about them, but not anymore. She realises now - when people behave negatively, i.e. they appear unkind or mean, they have their misunderstandings about how life works.

To resolve conflicts and differences in viewpoints, we can't insist that others see our way and try to argue our case. If we do so, they'll only build thicker walls of resistance, and we'd lose our opportunity to have meaningful conversations.

To resolve differences, we'll need to meet people where they are, setting aside our views and listening without judgements. When we do that, our mind will get quieter. When we are quiet and genuinely listen, that allows the other person to be less defensive too. In that space, better conversations are possible. Conflicts will seem easier to resolve in that dynamic.

Conflicts may not always resolve though, especially if both parties have a vested interest in sticking to their points of view that are fundamentally different. There'll be times when it may be best to agree to disagree and make a decision that makes sense. Sometimes, a higher-level conflict between people in an organisation may require formal or informal mediation. Again, any attempts at reconciliation would work best when both parties understand how the mind works and where individual experiences come from.

For Hannah, the biggest difference she noticed in herself since learning this understanding, was her relationship with other professionals within her multidisciplinary team.

'I'm able to listen to what makes sense to that clinician. If I disagree, I'm able to talk about how I saw things differently, and that isn't as confrontational or conflicting as it might have been in the past.'

Hannah feels less defensive about her practice. She accepts that she and everyone else can make mistakes and get things wrong, and that was all okay as long as they learned from it.

Part FOUR

Frequently Asked Questions

Can my boss and colleagues make me feel stressed?

The answer is no, your boss and colleagues can't make you feel stressed, no matter how convinced you are.

Consciousness *seduces* you into believing your thoughts – that the people around you at work or elsewhere are making you stressed.

Both Shelly and Mike used to think that other people at work (colleagues and boss, respectively) could make them feel stressed. Having had profound insights (realisations), about the powerful workings of *mind, thought and consciousness,* they no longer believe that to be true.

Are you saying that I should allow other people in power to use me 'as a doormat'?

Absolutely not. I'm not implying you do nothing about the *issues* you face at work. I'm also not giving an opinion about whether other people's actions are right or wrong.

I'm pointing you to the fact that the only way you can experience life, including circumstances at work or people in power, is via the power of thought.

When you realise this at a deeper level, you'll be able to bounce back from setbacks sooner than later. You'll start to access fresh thoughts and ideas that will help you resolve the challenges you face, and decisions you need to make.

In each story in this book, there's one thing in common – each person has felt empowered rather than disempowered after learning how the mind works.

So, am I the one making myself stressed?

Yes, but please hear this -

You're making yourself stressed because of an innocent misunderstanding on your part as to where your feelings come from one hundred percent of the time.

As long as you believe that your experience of stress (or any other feeling) is coming from the outside world, i.e. your work circumstances or work colleagues and not from the power of thought taking form in the moment, you'll continue to attribute your feelings to something outside of you.

You'll continue to feel at the mercy of the external world.

As soon as you have a glimpse of how the mind works and how you (and everyone else) experience life and the world around you, feelings of stress and overwhelm will have a weaker grip on you.

Nothing outside (of you) will have necessarily changed, and yet you'll begin to feel different from the inside. That's what it felt like to all the individuals who share their powerful stories of transformation here.

And, it's not about feeling guilty or blaming yourself for *causing* stress in the first place. You'll notice that even feelings of guilt or blame are temporary and are nothing more than personal thoughts. As most people have shared, they still get tricked into believing their stressful thinking at times. I do too!

Can I practice meditation or mindfulness to alleviate feelings of stress and anxiety at work?

By all means, you can keep doing whatever works for you as long as it's a healthy enjoyable practice. But, as already mentioned, even if you don't practice any tools or techniques, including meditation or mindfulness, you're still connected to *a space of health and well-being at your core*. Remember — *the yolk is already in the egg!*

It's this space that people who meditate, practice yoga or mindfulness touch when engaged in those practices. It's important to note that this space is always there, even when we don't experience it at all or when we're feeling stressed and burned out.

But, I have a diagnosis of mental health/physical health issues that hinder me being my best at work.

Yes, certain factors and conditions can affect your physiological state. For example, you may feel tired or drowsy because of your health issues or experience side-effects from medication. Your pain and discomfort may trouble you and make it hard to focus at work. Your health problems can contribute to a range of other problems that may interfere with your ability to do your job well.

I'm not saying that you haven't got any problems and that your experiences aren't real. As always, thought still plays a huge part. The only way you can appreciate your physical or emotional health issue is via thought. And you can also have thinking about your thinking, for example: 'I shouldn't be thinking this.'

When excessive thinking settles down, it has less of a burdening effect on your physiological and psychological state. You may continue to need the support to be in place for you. This support could mean different things for different people – it might be about cutting down the number of hours and going part-time; for others, it might be about taking things gently and making time for regular breaks.

However, the less you're bothered by your thinking because you understand where your experiences are coming from, the easier it'll be for you to do your job well.

After returning to work, following a period of sickness absence, Shelly's mental health started to deteriorate once again. She was diagnosed with clinical depression, and she started taking antidepressant medication. It was around this time that she came across the principles behind innate health and resilience and had a powerful insight – that *the thoughts in my head are made up*. She has since managed to come off antidepressant medication, continued to be well and thrive at work.

Shelly says she has never felt so mentally healthy in years. She's confident that given what she knows now, she may still have the occasional bad day or hour and feel low from time to time, but she's confident she'll never return to the 'same horrible, dark place' of some years ago.

It's important to point out that everyone's different. Not everyone suffering from clinical depression or any other mental health condition may benefit from this understanding as much as Shelly has (or benefit at all).

However, everyone, irrespective of whether they have a particular health condition or not, whether they go to work or not, will continue to suffer if they

don't understand how the mind works and
innocently continue to misuse the power of thought.

Part FIVE

Beyond Coping Strategies

12

Thriving when the going is tough

*"What stops people from achieving
their goals is not a lack of resources,
but a lack of resourcefulness."*
– ANTHONY ROBBINS

Sometimes, people feel that they've lost their passion for work because of excessive workload and increasing demand on their time.

Reigniting the lost interest and passion for your work is possible.

Despite scarce resources and other challenges at work, there could be an infinite number of possibilities and opportunities still available to you. The more you see the truth of this, the more helpful thoughts and ideas you'll have access to.

Feelings are our friends – yes, all of them, even the ones that we don't like to feel such as stress and anxiety. They turn our *internal stress alarm* (i.e. stress response) system on, to warn us that something needs to be tended to.

Usually, the alarm cuts off once the threat or problem (either real or perceived) is dealt with. If we overanalyse and hang onto the thought that had triggered the stress alarm, we will cause our stress response system to remain activated – that, in turn, negatively impacts our overall state of mind, physical and emotional well-being.

Once we understand the power of thought and the innocent misuse of this power by overthinking, it doesn't make sense to keep the stress response switched on for long. We simply get on with work knowing - we're okay, no matter what!

With far fewer things on her mind that she pays attention to, Jane now gets more done at work. She's able to tap into her creativity and resourcefulness most of the time. Despite her busy work schedule in an acute hospital ward, she has found innovative ways to connect with her patients and staff.

Just like Jane, Shelly also has found her understanding of the principles helpful in her role as a senior manager. She's using that for mentoring and supervision, delivering sessions on innate resilience and also leading change projects.

Even if one continues to work in a demanding environment, it's still possible to thrive and feel well in the workplace.

Samaira says: 'Laughter and smiles are filling my work rather than stress and self-judgment, something I used to feel on a regular basis. It has helped me tremendously to learn that feelings come from within.'

Mike says: 'I can walk into my office and have a really lovely peaceful feeling, something I had never experienced at work before. I am considerably calmer. My colleagues say I am smiling more, that I take things in my stride, something no one had ever said to me.'

Shelly says: 'At work, people soon started noticing the transformation in me. I no longer felt stressed out, at least not for long, the work environment started to flourish, and the relationships began to feel *more human*.'

Hannah says: 'I don't plan as I used to. I trust *mind* and that it will guide me to say what I need to say in sessions. This way work is hundred times better and more enjoyable. I understand the implication of the theory I was taught 12 years ago. Before it was just a nice concept, but now I understand what my teachers were trying to teach me; I'm more awake and much more open-minded.'

13

Taking time off work

Sometimes, people feel guilty about taking time off work. They fear being judged by their colleagues and also worry about letting others down.

And, it may well be the case that others judge you or that you feel judged by them. That's what happened in Shelly's case. You can't stop people from having judgmental thoughts about you. Even you can't *stop you* from ever having judgmental thoughts, from feeling guilt, fear, worry or any emotions for that matter.

Guilt feelings come from guilt-laden thoughts at any given moment. It's impossible to feel guilty all the time. That feeling will wax and wane as the idea takes form and disappears again.

Fearful feelings about being judged come from fearful thoughts about being judged. It's impossible to feel nervous about being judged all the time. That feeling will vary too as the thought takes form and disappears again.

In the same way, worrying feelings about letting others down come from worrying thoughts about letting others down. It's impossible to feel worried about letting others down all the time. That feeling will wax and wane as the thought takes form and disappears again.

I hope, by now, you have spotted the *thought-created-reality* (TCR) patterns in the context of taking time off work.

A break from regular work is needed when one is feeling extremely stressed and unable to cope with demands of their job. It allows the person to have a much-needed respite from the pressures of a regular, work routine, to reflect on their experiences, to re-energise, to recover, until ready to return.

14

Returning to Work

If you've been off work for a while and dreading going back, worried how you might cope with the work pressure, anxious about getting started again, about facing your colleagues and clients, you might find it useful to reflect on your experiences and what I've shared in this book.

I've worked with individuals who had been off work due to stress. When it's time to return to their jobs, the common fear is of suffering yet another emotional breakdown from stress and anxiety.

As a coach, my job is to guide them to the truth that they are designed to feel their thinking in the moment – and, that they couldn't control how they'd feel when they returned to work.

Once you realise that you can't predict or control what thoughts come to you at any moment, understand that you're innately resilient (even though you may not feel it), you'll find it easier to relax. Returning to work will seem much easier than you had previously anticipated.

Part SIX

People's Stories

*"Knowing others is wisdom,
knowing yourself is
enlightenment."*
- Lao-tse

15

Thoughts in the head are actually made up – Shelly's story

Shelly is a career woman, a wife and a mother of four. She's a registered general nurse (RGN) and has been working in the NHS for around 20 years. She has always been a lateral thinker and passionate about finding innovative ways to improve existing services and designing new ones. She became a senior manager very early on in her career. She'd described herself in the past as a 'workaholic', driven by results and at times in her career working 60 hours a week for 'as long as I can remember'.

About ten years ago, she received a promotion at work and landed a new senior management job which she found very busy and extremely stressful.

It was a newly designed post, and to give people an idea of what the demands of her new job were like, she said: 'Now ten people at my level are employed to do what I was originally employed to do.' Around the same time as landing with the new job, she became pregnant and went on maternity leave within the first year of securing this new post.

When she came back from maternity leave, she found her job extremely challenging and was working long hours with such demands that left her feeling that she couldn't cope. About seven years ago, she experienced severe stress and burnout in the workplace and had to go on sick leave. She was off work for nearly four months.

When she returned to work, she had a difficult time with some of her colleagues. She felt judged by them that despite being in such a senior leadership position, she had been 'off with stress'. Her occupational health department was adamant that she cut down some of her responsibilities and hours at work. This meant she had to give up a lot of her previous commitments and received some backlash from her peers.

Their attitude towards her seemed to be one of disapproval for not being able to handle things at work and for management agreeing to reduce her workload. Shelly felt labelled at work. Shelly found all these difficult to handle, and she had to move her office space and keep a distance from them 'just to protect me'. As the interpersonal relationship with her colleagues continued to be difficult alongside other factors at work, Shelly found her mental health deteriorating again and noticed the signs and symptoms of stress and burnout returning.

That was about three years since her last breakdown. 'I tried to keep my head above the water, but it got too much.'

Shelly sought advice and support from her GP and occupational health and was advised to take time off work. Shelly decided against it, though. The organisation was going through another major change, and she felt that if she were to take time off work, she could be blamed for several things that were happening at the time. 'After all the work I had done over the years I was not prepared to disappear and allow it to happen.' Shelly confided that she was struggling to such an extent by then that the only way she could turn up at work was by taking diazepam on a regular basis to calm her nerves. At one point, she was crying all the time. Her GP and occupational health were aware of that, as Shelly tried to maintain full attendance at work. The threat of a restructure again within the organisation meant that any sick leave could be used against a staff member when reallocating new positions in the future.

Shelly filled in an online questionnaire, and the results implied that she could be clinically depressed. She discussed this with her GP, as up until this time she was reluctant to take any medication and had tried various other strategies to try and manage stress, e.g. walking, jogging, yoga, massage etc. Her GP prescribed her an antidepressant. Shelly said she hated taking the medication the first time but decided to give it a go, mainly for the sake of her family, but promised herself that she would come off it in a year's time. She did start to feel better gradually. Although she had planned to stop antidepressant medication after a year, because of some ill-health in the wider family, Shelly and her GP agreed to continue with the medication for another six months.

Around that time, Shelly started to look at self-help approaches to well-being and read several books on this topic. She accidentally stumbled across the principles of innate health and resilience. Curious to find out more, Shelly attended a weekend boot camp event / retreat in London in February 2016. By the second day of the retreat, she had a huge insight into the nature of human experiences and the fact that thoughts in the head are made up. She got extremely emotional and tearful as she realised in an instant that it was true. By the end of the day, she felt exhausted but also felt lighter in herself.

Soon after that, Shelly started noticing that she was 'overly happy' and decided to come off her antidepressant, which she has been able to do successfully. She has remained well since and says she never felt so mentally healthy in years. During the time from her first major insight to coming off medication, Shelly started to see the thought-feeling connection; she realised that if she didn't take her negative thoughts seriously then negative feelings would reduce too. The thought-feeling connection made sense to Shelly, and she tried and tested that on many occasions. She also started to share her new understanding and experience with her husband and children at home.

'At work, people soon started noticing the transformation in me. I no longer feel stressed out, at least not for long.'

Shelly noticed an improvement in her team, which was a multi-disciplinary team of surgeons and other healthcare professionals. 'In my department, the work environment started to flourish, and the relationships began to feel more human.'

Her colleagues noticed Shelly's transformation and sought her out to have informal chats about their worries and concerns. She continued her journey outside of her healthcare job and completed a year-long programme of coach training in September 2017. Her coach training was underpinned by principles about how the mind works.

Although her role doesn't involve coaching people at work, Shelly has found her training extremely helpful at a personal level as well as for her role at the hospital. She has been able to use those skills for mentoring and supervision, delivering sessions on resilience and leading change projects. She feels much calmer and content at work. She now maintains a balanced life, keeping close to her contracted hours, but seems to get more things done without spending long hours at work.

Although she may still have the occasional bad day or hour and feel low from time to time, Shelly is confident that given what she knows now, that she will never return to the dark periods of a few years ago.

Shelly reflected on how she used to dread meeting some of her colleagues who she felt had been unkind to her in the past, but not any longer. She can now see through the thought illusions that get in the way of clear thinking about what's true.

Shelly used to have a lot of judgemental thoughts about her colleagues, but not anymore. She often notices that she has compassion for them as they, too, get stuck within their thought illusions. She realises that she also created many stories in the past, and replayed thoughts and events in her mind. She knows that: 'when people behave negatively (i.e. they appear unkind or mean), they have their misunderstandings about how life works.'

Shelly feels more authentic than ever before. 'I show up as I am. I don't have to put a mask on and go to work.' She's found this incredibly liberating and enjoys work much more than she used to.

As a senior manager, it has been constructive for her to see past people's bad behaviour to the fact that they are acting out of insecurity. Because she sees this, she's able to listen to their concerns, reach out and help them. Shelly referred to a couple of lines in a book that she read, during this journey, that has also had an impact on her.

'Bad behaviour is people acting out of insecurity; if we see this as wilful, we tend to want to control and punish, but if we see this bad behaviour as people acting out of insecurity then we tend to want to help them.'

Shelly thanked Jack Pransky for that quote that allowed her to see that for herself, both at work and in her life as a parent.

16

A shift will take place – Jane's story

Jane is a mental health and general nurse by background. She works as a ward manager in an acute psychiatric inpatient unit for adults. The work environment can be an extremely busy one. There is a lot of pressure on making beds available, and pressure to get people better swiftly and to discharge them without unnecessary delays. Some of her responsibilities include managing the day-to-day tasks of the ward, managing clinical governance issues, ensuring that a high standard of care is delivered to patients, offering a safe, timely and recovery-oriented service, providing staff supervision and appraisal, and managing safe-staffing levels, staff sickness and performance.

Jane said that before having this understanding, her emotional response tended to be on the extreme side. 'I always felt that things were either very personally directed or that I had to defend things,' she confessed. These intense emotional responses would also last for several hours, if not longer.

For instance, if she was in a business meeting, and people were unable to understand what she was trying to explain and they were defensive, Jane would get defensive too. 'I wouldn't be fully present in the business meeting, and wouldn't be able to hear them. I'd get anxious, almost be frozen by anxiety at times, although outwardly that wouldn't show.'

After such a meeting experience, she would routinely analyse what had happened, how it went, who said what and went over minute details over and over in her head. Jane would then dread going to the next meeting.

With the new understanding of where her experiences come from all the time, Jane still tends to feel anxious and emotional; these are nothing compared to her past experience in terms of intensity and prolonged suffering.

Rather than immediately getting defensive or annoyed, if she perceives someone as objecting to her viewpoint or challenging the proposed change in practice, she is now able to listen and respond to their concerns most of the time. Jane said: 'My understanding has shifted, and I see that the person is coming from a place of fear; that they're thinking of how is it going to affect them. So, I'm able to explain it much more calmly and responsibly, listen and not take it so personally.'

Jane admits: 'I still feel stressed, but I'm much more aware of it. I'm able to name it and take responsibility for it.'

Jane also felt that with far fewer things on her mind to carry around, she was getting more things done and was able to be more creative and resourceful most of the time.

Previously, if she was in the midst of some important work in her office and staff or patients came in wanting her time, Jane would struggle. 'In the past, I felt I needed to please people and ensure I did the best I could. I couldn't say no. I didn't look after myself.' She tended to stay at work late or take her work home because she hadn't had the time to complete them. That obviously had a negative impact on her personal and family life.

Now, Jane can lay down some boundaries at work and be helpful at the same time. 'If someone asks for my time and I'm doing something, I tell them that I'd love to have some time with them but that they would need to wait for when I'm able to give them time.' People seem to be okay with that, and she feels that's helped a lot. 'Then, when I'm with the person, I can connect with them. They tend to leave (my office) much quicker because they feel heard; I get the time to finish what I need to do.'

Jane had always worked in a creative and recovery-oriented way. She has created a quiet sanctuary in her office. On a busy acute inpatient ward, staff and patients come to her office, sometimes looking for a quiet space. Patients have said to her: 'It's quiet in here (i.e. her office).' She welcomes them in, and she asks permission to carry on with whatever she needs to do. Patients sometimes come in and sit quietly in her office. At times, they may write or draw something. When Jane gets time, they may get into a conversation about books and read a few pages of poetry together. 'I always used to do things like this, but I feel I've much more connectedness with it now than before. In the past, I did it to fix, to do something. Now, the shift for me is that it's not about me, it's about the person. It's about offering a space where the person feels connected to themselves.'

Jane notices her ego at play at work, not just some of the time, but often. She has also begun to be aware of her body when she feels stressed. 'I used to be very much in my head. Now with the understanding, I feel a sick feeling in my stomach, and I notice it.' She takes this as a reminder that she is getting caught up in her thinking. Her level of self-awareness has improved. She notices that she tends to get stressed and frustrated when tired or hungry. She listens to what her body needs. Sometimes, she catches herself getting judgemental thoughts about the system and other people. She's able to step back and do something different, like go out for a short walk or get out of the unit to take some fresh air. These are strategies available to anyone. For Jane, these practical strategies come more naturally now. She realises that she doesn't have to do anything unique to fix her thinking. She's aware of the role of thought in creating her experiences and the fact that her experiences would change naturally as her thinking changes. She's also mindful of the fact that fresh thoughts and ideas are available to her even when she isn't actively seeking.

With this understanding, Jane can be in touch with her innate well-being and more often than not. She is also able to point people to their resilience as best as she can.

She now tends to be less judgemental about staff. She feels she can listen better now. 'It's not that I don't do my job, which could be about absence management or if other difficulties need addressing. I'm able to do that, but I'm able to hear what they (staff) say to me in a more meaningful way. It might not change the outcome, but the process is different. The understanding is on a much better level, and I don't take it as much personally.'

On the whole, Jane feels she is much more productive at work and has more space to be creative. She's able to use her common sense more and is fascinated by how her wisdom shows up guiding her to do the best she can despite any challenges. She shares this understanding in her way, in a way that makes sense to people. Operating from this understanding have helped her staff-team in also using their creativity to support patients in distress.

They're able to bring compassionate care to their practice, despite everyday challenges of working within a busy environment.

17

Sense of empowerment – Mike's story

Mike has been working as a counsellor for several years. A year ago, Mike had to take time off work due to stress. He had difficulties with his manager, whom he perceived as caring more about the senior leadership team, ignoring the team he was managing and the people they were serving. Mike recalls feeling overwhelmed with stress and anxiety. It seemed as if the team were given more and more targets to achieve over time, and everyone was struggling.

He spoke up about what he thought was wrong with the system, but he did it in a way which backfired. He recalls feeling livid and reacting to an email from the service manager thanking the team for hitting all the targets. Mike was furious, as he felt the message should have been about the need to meaningfully help service users rather than about motivating people to achieve more targets. Without even pausing to consider the consequences of reacting in such a way, he wrote an email response back speaking his mind. It didn't go down well. In the end, he took sick leave for several months as he felt quite stressed out and overwhelmed.

On his return, he was moved to another team within the same service but under a different manager. He continued to feel resentment about what had happened, how the service provision was still stretched and patchy. Most of all, he dreaded meeting the service manager.

Soon after his return, quite fortunately, he was introduced to the principles of innate health and resilience. 'This is the best thing I've ever come across,' he said. He got an insight into the transient nature of thought. He realised that without him doing anything, his thoughts and feelings would change.

Mike had used food to cope with stress in the past and had developed an eating disorder. He had two coping strategies to deal with his stress. The healthy strategy was running, and the unhealthy one was to get obsessed about cleaning (he had suffered from OCD in the past). After coming home from work, he would get routinely stressed about how things were untidy at home, and then act on this feeling by making sure he cleaned up everything as soon as he reached home. He hardly took any rest and was constantly ruminating about events at his workplace.

Once he got the understanding, Mike's experience of work and the workplace changed overnight. He saw that people within his organisation were doing the best they could, given what they believed to be true and what was expected of them. He saw that he didn't need his work or other people to change, for him to feel better. He no longer dreaded meeting with the service manager and was pleasantly surprised with how calm he felt when he did bump into him. 'I felt okay. I didn't feel intimidated. I didn't feel worried. I was able to go past what had happened.'

Mike still gets caught up in his thinking about how bad some things are in his organisation. However, there has been a shift. 'I still think all that, but it doesn't hang around for that long. I still don't like the way things are in the organisation as a whole, but I acknowledge this is how things are in the moment. I do get angry but accept that I'm a human being and have different experiences, including experiences of anger.' He's also aware that his negative experiences of the workplace are not generated by the managers, by the system or other reasons but by his thinking about all that.

He added: 'I can choose to get caught up in all that, but it makes me more stressed and more bitter. Or, I can carry on doing the best I can. Knowing this gives me a sense of empowerment – it is incredibly empowering.'

Knowing that his experiences are generated internally via thought in the moment meant he no longer needed to *fix* the situation or change other people's behaviour to feel better in the moment.

He adds: 'I can sit with my feelings much better. I know they'll pass, perhaps not as fast as I want them to but they'll pass. It's less hard work.' He feels much calmer and happier at work, grateful for being able to do what he does instead of focusing on what's wrong with the system.

'I can walk into my office and have a beautiful, peaceful feeling, something I've never experienced at work before. I am considerably calmer. My colleagues say I am smiling more, that I take things in my stride, something no one ever told me before.'

He feels much more able to look after himself. He doesn't worry about not meeting targets and, in the process, doesn't get overwhelmed. 'I'll do my best, but I don't have to worry about not meeting them. If it happens for some reason, it happens. Even if I don't manage to meet my target in a week but managed to get everything else done, if I felt calmer and my thinking has been clearer, that to me is success.'

Looking back prior to his coming across the principles behind innate health and resilience, Mike remarks, 'I used to do everything very quickly. I walked everywhere quickly. I spoke quickly. Everything had to be done quickly. It was like I was on some drug. Other members of my team and I used to moan and complain a lot about the various challenges at work.' That fuelled more thoughts of anger and frustration. It didn't change the situation. If anything, it made people feel worse.

Mike still has contact with his former colleagues – who tell him about their ongoing unhappiness at work. 'It's like they are expecting me to open my big mouth like last year and then send off an email,' he grins. He chooses to ignore the emails, as he feels he doesn't need to fuel their frustrations anymore. 'It doesn't serve them or me.'

Mike concludes, 'I have my moments, but I know that's just my *human experience*. I often tell myself, "You don't have to believe your thinking," and I smile at myself because I genuinely believe that now.'

18

Switching off from work mode –

Hannah's story

Hannah has been working as a therapist in the NHS for over a decade in specialist mental health services.

Prior to coming to this understanding, she'd sometimes worry about her patients and take those worries home. She doubted whether she was a *good enough* practitioner. Like many in her profession, she had a lot to do in a limited amount of time. She used to rush around and spend time worrying that she would not complete all the tasks she had.

Hannah used to feel responsible for her patients getting better, and for their well-being. When her patients recovered, she thought it was because of her therapy work and vice-versa. She believed that it was up to her to find solutions for her patients, taking full responsibility to alleviate their suffering. That led her to put a lot of pressure on herself.

Since coming across the principles of innate health and resilience a few years ago, several things have changed for Hannah at work as well as at home. She now feels better focused on her tasks and very rarely feels overwhelmed. She says: 'It may sound simple, but I know that I can only do what I can do in the moment, that the more attention I give to my thinking, that I have x, y and z to do before I go home, the less easily I'll be able to do x, y and z.'

Hannah recognises that if she's feeling stressed then it's because she entertains thoughts like 'you're never going to get this done,' 'you are not good at this' or, 'you are not good at time keeping' and believing those thoughts to be true.

The biggest difference this understanding has made for her is a new trust in her ability to handle differences within the multidisciplinary team and the way she sees each clinician's perspective when they are all supporting the same patient.

Hannah talks about how she had felt defensive about her practice in the past, not wanting to get things wrong. 'I'm not self-conscious in the same way I was,' she says. 'I do get things wrong, and that's okay which means I can have conversations with colleagues that I might not have welcomed or been receptive to in the past. Now, as patients go through one part of the treatment to another, I don't take ownership of their recovery or get defensive. I can reflect on what we're not doing together that to help the patient rather than judge each other.'

Hannah also realises that, 'how well people are doing doesn't have anything to do with me as a practitioner.' She now understands that the primary reason people got better following therapy was because of the personal insights and understanding they had. Hannah realised that people had to see something for themselves and find their answers.

'The safer a place I can make for them to have an insight and point them back to their wisdom and common sense, the more I can help the patient see that they are their best therapist.' Hannah is clearly more confident as a therapist because she now understands where her own and her patient's experiences come from.

'I don't plan as much as I used to. I trust *mind* and that it will guide me to say what I need to say in sessions. This way of working is a hundred times better and more enjoyable. I understand the implication of the theory I learned 12 years ago. Before it was more of an *ideal concept* or a *nice theory*, but now I understand what my teachers were trying to teach me about intuition, the guide inside, the *treasures* within each person. I'm more awake and much more open-minded.'

Hannah feels much more confident as a therapist and the ways she can support her patients. Changes in the workplace have meant that she has had to take on additional responsibilities. In the past, she would have had anxious thinking about doing more complicated tasks; as her mind seems clearer, she feels in a better position to take on new challenges. As appropriate and when the need arises, Hannah asks for guidance from colleagues and her supervisor to validate her work. Insecure thinking doesn't bother her for long because she is now able to recognise it for what it is, and ultimately, she knows that things will be okay. She now concentrates more on her practice, and has found that her productivity levels have increased.

Hannah no longer feels the need to carry work issues home. Once she has finished work, she now finds it easier to switch off from work and gets to truly enjoy her evenings and weekends with her family.

19

No longer responsible for other's

actions – Samaira's story

Samaira is an interior design consultant and works in a design firm. She acknowledges that work can feel stressful, especially in a sales and target driven environment. 'Meeting deadlines and managing multiple areas of work require an organised diary, ability to focus on the task at hand and manage time wisely,' she says.

She has come across the principles behind innate health and resilience only very recently, and although new to this understanding, she has already noticed a huge difference when it comes to experiencing stress and overwhelm in the workplace. The following is her story in her own words.

'As a career woman for the last 18 years or so, I've worked in different work environments. I've seen several changes at various levels in the workplace, and all those had an impact on my job roles and expectations from me at work. I've faced several challenges. The biggest challenge of all has been to be calm in any given environment, no matter how chaotic things get, review the situation and resolve it.

'Before I came to this understanding, the challenges at work were taking a toll on me. I used to feel stressed and overwhelmed, and those episodes used to last a long time. I used to feel bitter and restless at work and bring those feelings home with me.

'Just to give an example, once I was taking care of some high-level issues in the absence of higher management, something that required a lot of attention to detail and execution of decisions. That was above and beyond my role and responsibility. In the heat of the situation, my stress levels rose, and unfortunately, I carried it back home too. I ignored the beautiful smiles on my kids' faces. I was too negative and kept them at a distance. It lasted a few days and eventually, I grew out of it. It felt very bitter, though.

'Since having an understanding of the principles, I feel more aware of my experiences and where they are coming from. I'm still working in the same environment and with the same people, but it feels as if I'm not the same person anymore. Despite constant pressure and targets imposed on us, I feel calmer and in control of myself. I know I'm not responsible for other people's actions and that my actions may not always deliver hundred percent results as expected, and that's still okay.

'Laughter and smiles are filling my work time, rather than stress and self-judgment that I used to feel on a regular basis. It has helped me tremendously to learn that feelings come from within and I now share what I've learned with others.'

20

Feeling low is no longer a scary place – Phil's story

Phil is a surgeon and works full-time in the NHS. As you can imagine, his work can be pretty hectic. He had always been interested not only in improving his core surgical skills to do his day job well but also in enhancing his soft skills, skills he felt would help to improve his performance and productivity, improve communication, and help build rapport with his patients and colleagues. He had earlier explored sports psychology and various self-help approaches, including neuro-linguistic programming (NLP).

About three years ago, after taking on several additional leadership roles at work, Phil experienced symptoms of burnout, and in his own words: 'I simply couldn't cope anymore.' He believed without a shadow of a doubt that the cause of his stress and burnout was external and that, 'I can't work efficiently unless the entire system changes.' He acknowledged feeling like a victim and that he hated being in that position. He resigned from his several of his leadership roles and started focusing on his core work. Phil said: 'This was enough to de-pressurise my psychological environment.'

Around the same time, he came across two books: *Clarity* by Jamie Smart, and *The Inside-out Revolution* by Michael Neill. As Phil delved into the content of those, he realised that both the books were pointing to something beyond strategies and techniques. He realised that his resilience was not affected by external circumstances. He has since trained as a coach to help others overcome similar challenges and improve performance in the workplace.

Phil's still practising as a surgeon, and his job can be very hectic at times. Having this understanding has helped him work as best as he can, despite the finite resources available to him, not letting anxious thoughts get in the way. He feels that there are systems that need to be improved. However, not ruminating about what could be better within the system is not about being in denial about the need to improve things. He realised that his time would be much better invested if he took his concerns and ideas for change along to company meetings and forums engaged in service innovation and redesign, rather than ruminating about *the problems* anytime and anywhere.

He now finds it easier to step back and refrain from problem-solving in the heat of the moment. He's more able to focus on and deal with what's important and in front of him.

Another thing that has shifted is Phil's previous fear of his own emotions and other people's emotions. He felt he didn't know how to handle those. He used to believe that the fewer emotions one experienced at work the better. 'My emotions still go up and down. I still find myself in situations where I feel low. But they're different from before, in that it's not a scary place because I know it's temporary. And, I know from experience that unless I look for the cause of my feelings on the outside, and unless I try to fix the situation on the outside to fix the feeling, I know that my thought will flow and my feelings will flow with the thought. I find myself in a different place!'

FINAL THOUGHTS

"If aught I have said is truth, that
truth shall reveal itself in a clearer
voice, and in words more kin to
your thoughts."
- Kahlil Gibran

Thank you so much for taking the time to read this book!

Are you intrigued by what you've read and curious to find out more?

Does the message in the book make sense to you at some level or, are you confused about some of the contents? Or, perhaps your intellect is finding it hard to grasp the logic presented in this book. If so, I'm with you on this one.

When I first got introduced to this understanding about five years ago, through my husband (who's also a psychiatrist), I was sceptical. I thought this was something I had always known as a psychiatrist but was *packaged* differently.

I figured it was a bit like CBT (Cognitive Behavioural Therapy) and a bit of mindfulness. I was obviously wrong, but my intellect made it hard for me to accept that it was any different to some of the traditional self-help approaches.

I didn't get that it wasn't an approach and that it was an entirely different paradigm in contrast to the self-help paradigm I knew. As a psychiatrist trainee, I'd trained in CBT (cognitive behaviour therapy), psychodynamic psychotherapy, cognitive analytical therapy, family and solution-focused therapies. I had also trained as a practitioner in various coaching modalities – life coaching, NLP (Neuro-linguistic Programming), narrative coaching and EFT (Emotional Freedom Techniques). I was a certified and accredited EFT trainer training people to become EFT practitioners. My coaching practice was primarily around helping people change their negative feelings and states by using various tools from my coaching *toolbox*. I'd assist them to reframe their negative beliefs and thoughts into positive ones, focus on strategies to achieve their goals to help them feel better about themselves. It's no wonder that I initially found it hard to *grasp this understanding (of innate health and well-being)*.

I was oblivious that the mind only worked one way — that we all lived in a *thought-generated-reality* all the time. It hadn't dawned on me that we all had access to innate well-being and resilience, even if we didn't feel it or believed that to be true.

It took me about six months to move from a place of intellectually understanding *this concept* to having an *aha* moment, a realisation from within. I saw then that it wasn't an approach or an idea. It was a new paradigm about how the mind works.

And that realisation has been a game changer for me.

There's no way I could've planned my moment of insight. It happened during a coaching session, but it could have happened anytime. As the years passed, I've had more insights that have guided me immensely. I'm very fortunate to share what little I know with people and see their lives changing.

Life (and work as an independent psychiatrist and wellness coach) has begun to feel simpler and more meaningful.

And yes, I still get caught up in my thinking!

And thank goodness, I see it more clearly now than ever before.

If you feel drawn to learn more, I encourage you to explore the Three Principles understanding of innate health and resilience in a bit more depth than I was able to provide in this book.

In the next section, you'll find a list of books and online resources that I have found useful. You'll also find an up-to-date list of helpful publications and videos in the resource section of our website - https://ranibora.com

Finally, I hope you'll give yourself permission to enjoy the ebb and flow of your ever-changing emotional states knowing that deep within you, you are okay.

Remember – *'the yolk is already in the egg…'*

So, this is all from me for now. I wish you fun and the very best in life – at work, in business and your relationships. Please remember, some days you are bound to struggle, and on other days you'll surprise yourself by what you are innately capable!

What if George Pransky was right when he redefined stress as: '...*nothing more than the weight of negative thinking taken seriously over time.*'

It's time to turn stress on its head!

With warmest regards,

Rani

Website: https://ranibora.com

Email: support@ranibora.com

Twitter: @ranibora

RESOURCES

Books I can recommend:

Second Chance, by Sydney Banks

The Enlightened Gardener, by Sydney Banks

The Missing Link, by Sydney Banks

The Inside-Out Revolution, by Michael Neill

Coming Home, by Dicken Bettinger & Natasha Swerdloff

One Thought Changes Everything, by Mara Gleason

The Little Book of Clarity, by Jamie Smart

Exquisite Mind, by Terry Rubenstein

Invisible Power, by Ken Manning, Robin Charbit and Sandra Krot

The Serenity Principle, by Joe Bailey

Websites I can recommend:

http://www.3pgc.com

http://www.threeprinciplesfoundation.org

http://www.threeprinciplesmovies.com

http://innatehealth.co/london-centre

Acknowledgements

Firstly, I'd like to acknowledge and thank my friend and GP colleague, Dr Nimita Gandhi for sowing the seed for this book.

Thank you to the six beautiful souls who have shared their personal stories of transformation achieved through the understanding of the principles (of innate health and well-being). The journey of this book wouldn't have been possible without your generous and selfless contribution. I'm very grateful!

I want to acknowledge Mary Schiller, for her help with the initial editing of the book. Thank you, Ian Watson - for your wise guidance and help with the back cover description. I'm grateful to you, Natasha Swerdloff and Liz Scott for the help and advice I had from you both!

I shall be forever grateful to all the Three Principles educators and teachers from whom I was fortunate to learn, either directly or indirectly.

The person I'm most indebted to is my dear friend, husband and fellow psychiatrist, Dr Suraj Gogoi. Without his unwavering support, constructive feedback, editing and creative skills, this book and the contents wouldn't have been the same.

Last but not the least, I'm incredibly grateful to the late Sydney Banks for sharing *this understanding* as best as he could - with love and simplicity…

About the Author

Dr Rani Bora is a holistic psychiatrist, mental health coach and international speaker. She has been a qualified medical doctor for the past twenty years, and currently a member of the Royal College of Psychiatrists, London. Rani had worked as a *consultant psychiatrist* in the NHS (of England, UK) engaged in the rehabilitation and recovery of younger adults with significant mental health problems. During that time, Rani had served as an associate clinical director and was a clinical lead for Schwartz Centre Rounds for NHS staff to promote compassionate care. Rani left her full-time NHS consultant position in 2016 to work independently, to pursue her passion for sharing the principles of innate health with a wider audience.

Rani has conducted numerous training for healthcare professionals and patients. She has co-facilitated several courses alongside individuals with lived experience of mental illness, and has published articles and booklets on *well-being, coaching for mental health recovery* and *empowering people.*

Visit https://ranibora.com for more details.

Printed in Great Britain
by Amazon

41248829R00104